FOLLIES

SARAH MARIA GRIFFIN

Belfast
LAPWING

First Published by Lapwing Publications
c/o 1, Ballysillan Drive
Belfast BT14 8HQ
lapwing.poetry@ntlworld.com
www.lapwingpoetry.com

Since before 1632
The Greig sept of the MacGregor Clan
Has been printing and binding books

All Lapwing Publications are
Printed and Hand-bound in Belfast
Set in Aldine 721 BT at the Winepress

ISBN 978-1-907276-69-9

ACKNOWLEDGEMENTS

I'd like to extend love to everyone who has helped me through advice and guidance and a push when I needed a push: Eva Bourke, Mia Gallagher, Stephen James Smyth and Colm Keegan, Sarah Clancy and Dani Gill (without their wise words the manuscript never would have been sent).

Love to those who have been close to me during the putting together of Follies: Lisa Keegan, Helena Egri (for the cover amongst many other things) and most of all, Ceri Bevan, for being muse, critic, provider of lasagne, and never ever embarrassed when people ask how he feels about being called a man-bride.

Love to Milk & Cookie Stories, love to North Beach Nights and Over the Edge, love to The BrownBread Mixtape, love to Nighthawks and Glór and every stage that's let me get up and say my poems into a microphone. Love to all of them because without them I'd probably have given up by now.

And last of all, love to the ghosts in the poetry and stories: to everyone who has come and gone and to everyone who stays, and makes my life the kind of life that I don't ever feel silly writing poetry about.

in my own words ... thank you
is a fuller 'thank you' to people I am grateful to
in so many ways and I need more than a simple list
to say so.

CONTENTS

FLASH PROSE

For Ma, Da, Katie & Nana Sheila,

Sure I didn't lick it off the stones

POETRY

crash

Let me climb in beside the crash of your body
and sleep by you
until all the hard steel and splintered glass of your exhausted form
is enveloped by the tender grassy roadside of the room where we landed
and my nighttime earth blanket folds over you and softens you
with mossy fingertips.

I awake no longer girl but tiger
drowsy and just ravenous now so
let me gnaw on you in this bed meadow off the motorway
leave little dents in you
my tiger teeth's signatures on you

no longer broken down
but ready to consume and be consumed.

Good morning, lover.

trampoline

He took pictures of me as I jumped
ONE TWO THREE
I held my knees
And then for a moment was a bad, bad shooting star
A comet in a Kodak flash

Oh yessir the boys with their telescopes and the men at Cape Kennedy
In the labs above the Rocket Gardens will stop and catch their
        breath as their hearts beat faster

You boys in white jackets observe, yes observe and be amazed
        as I crash towards your tiny planet
As I tear up your atmosphere and cascade towards your Earth
Where I will, in a second

(oh you never saw me coming i am a surprise greater than any new
        brother or sister)

Dive face first into and then upturn your blue sea, oh I will push
        up waves that will tear down skyscrapers
I will flood your homes, boys,
Unplug the television.

It will rain for six years
The ocean will become your sky and the air will be wet and smell
        like salt and seaweed
Whales I swear will fall and crush schools
Sharks will teethe on curbs of sidewalks

Tiny neons and angelfish will land in the Martini glasses of the
        rich, who remain,
Above the sodden ground.

lung

this is my thumb and index finger
and there is your earlobe between them
not the one with the freckle, the other -
(your head is on my chest) (lets make love)
this couch surrounds us and inside my tired head
it seems to rise and fall like us and our slow, synced breath
is thick with the heat of 40 LUCKY STRIKES
that we feel we never really wanted but
came with conversation, as always.
we have smoked too many cigarettes
and are now sitting in a big dark lung
alone but for the midnight taxis
and james bond on the television's screen
playing cards and failing to resuscitate his lover.

Marla Starr had two number one singles between 1970 and 1972

I haven't seen the future since 1976
And Christ I was getting old then

Looking out into a crowd of stoned faces with manky hair and
    smashed up teeth
Standing so tall in my rhinestone platforms I looked like a
    beautiful
Goddamned
Transvestite. I'd see right past all them headbangers and into the
    soul of God
Sure yeah I'd be singing and screaming covered in glitter and
    beads but
Fuck my mouth aint what mattered
It was my eyes
Penetrating through the masses and into outer fucking space, man

I saw shit you can't even imagine
All reaches of time and space
Birth, death, big steel birds
Towers falling
I saw great tidal waves piss on the Mardi Gras of the future

Lines of white off a schoolgirl's belly fuck I'm not even into girls
Or coke
I'm just into visions

Don't you call me a liar just look at my magnificent shoes
They are not shoes of a liar but of a fucking Godess with an eye
that sees all

Sometimes I walk around the house in them
And sing and hope to see these things again but damn all
happens.
My knees just get weak and the scars in my arms mock me
And tell me I'm a fool

this I have learned

Lust knows no words
Only tongues

i sprawl like a small dragon across your heart
crazy ex-boyfriend anecdotes swapped with an american

the first was this crazy hippie kid
a no shoes peter pan
with a palm tree in one hand
years and years of mysterious yellow notes on the porch
leading to going on tour with his terrible band
three years before the big split

but the internet makes you read and re-read forever
over chats and emails and skypes
(all these new words that don't sound right in a love poem)

how much heals while you sleep
and listen to alanis morisette songs
we wonder together

and then you fucking break their hearts for good decisions
and dancing
every
week

and when you have to leave for the other side of the world
the good choice boy just smiles and tells you
that travel invitations
are like
being asked to dance by god

moth

I really like the way you do things you're really not good at
All elbows and none of that ugly, boy pride
You're all experiment and fuck that if it doesn't work I'll try
        another way
You are smiling and indestructible
And fast food is just fine
Yeah, just fine tonight actually.

You'll clean my dishes afterwards you sweeter than sweet and sour
        boy
See, there's something you're never ever clumsy at
See, see,
You don't ever really break a thing when it matters
Even with your silly shaking hands, I trust you with my plates
And my heart, yeah, that too

You're late now and there is a moth in the room
I'm eating a Chinese alone and it's pathetic
Because we do this in our bed and fill the sheets with wild stray rice
High on MSG and laughing
Ignoring wayward insects that creep against white ceilings
Looking for the dark place behind the light

phenylthiocarbamide

Those cucumber slices are so inviting
round green watery lily-pad flat facemask eye-pieces
on top of the side salad next to your moussaka
I pick them off with my fingers because you think they taste sour
   and won't eat them
I murmur that you're wrong as I lick off the dressing and begin to
   eat them

You shake your head
looking down at your lunch
'No, I just know the truth.'

I stick one on the tip of my tongue and you tell me it's genetic
I whip it back into my mouth and feel a little sorry because you're
   missing out
'They taste like a little pond.'

'They're lying to you.' you reply with a quiet mouth
full of lettuce, lentils and broken tastebuds.

divine exodus part 1

I'm fighting back through a crowd in this big blue tent
Their faces are lit real bright as I elbow my way through
Their eyes all glassy and their bodies all dancing
And I'm walking out on them and whatever holy thing it is that
         shines on their bodies,
Rings in their ears

He calls me 'selectively claustrophobic';
I'm when I'm bored I just,
I just
Have to get out
So I excuse, sorry, can you let us, sorry, through there cheers

Like a grey fallen angel in the white light
Moving away from the music and out into the dark hush

divine exodus part 2

Think 30,000 burning tents

On my wrist they gave me some ribbon
With a black printed number and
"TOGETHER WE ARE ELECTRIC"
Together nothing
It's written on signs and banners
I am not part of your party
Your wet drunk grassy party
Don't fucking include me

I'm going to set it on fire
Find a team of fifty sober vagabonds
Who the party washes over but never touches
Something like pondwater on the feathers of some
Duck, swan, whatever
And we'll take our places
All around
Innocuously holding matches
And stolen petrol from Esso in Portlaoise.

Sore Mouth

I have an ulcer on the inside of my mouth that I keep tonguing
and can't help it

I think maybe I have an ulcer on my… on my soul
is that a rare thing
or an everybody's had it thing but nobody talks about it thing
maybe I should not tongue these memories and not like the little sting

and start using the strongest muscle in my body for loving

maybe kiss more
we should kiss more
let's kiss more

ulcers aren't contagious

are they

dublin soaks it up

Got on a 46a with only one story
Flew it in for once actually and I thought as I got to Leeson Street
Of other times different from this Tuesday

The seat throws me cause this bus is real close to the ground as we
        go over that bridge across the canal
And I'm suddenly back to the nights spent down this big road
Tanned legs and a cheap frock with a cigarette burn that you
        actually can't see through the rotten pattern
And that rise in the road unsettled a usually composed belly
Full with a bottle of wine and Smirnoff before I even left the
        house and went to the exhibition anyway

You look good
He said
That suit doesn't make you look like as much of a drug dealer as
I'd imagined
I said

Later standing by the tall gate near Sugar Club you know and
        threw up hard with a scarlet face
His identical twin brother taking a piss beside me with a smoke in
        his mouth

A blonde acquaintance held my hair and rubbed my back
Here don't worry love, happens to the best of us at the worst of times

this is a poem about three things
but mainly ikea

as we left for what your da called the badlands
the gate to our complex broke
and you licked the battery in the remote
and swore to me it'd work
that's how you bring them back to life
it did
but your tongue hurt then and tasted bad from the resurrection

four yellow letters
boom over the barren waste of this something like a suburb
this moth-eaten skyline
dwarfing the gold twinkle of the only taxi in the rank;
there was no room in the car after the grey billy shelves
the pots and pans of our new life

we were shattered
having walked miles through tunnels of
semi-disposable swedish furniture
and I think you nearly had a panic attack
and I think I made it worse
man up it's only furniture

there was no driver in the cab so we got the bus
and as we pulled out past musgroves your tongue still hurt
you stuck it out said at least it didn't taste like acid anymore
and I kissed you and it didn't

2008

The only meteor shower I ever watched
Was on the roof of a guy with a girlfriend's car
Up a hill outside a hotel
And it was real cold and we didn't talk
      except sometimes gasped at them
They streaked silver across the sky like it was being torn apart
By some big tiger that lived outside our universe
(striped none the less in orange and black)
Digging his sharp space-claws, one by one, into the inky canvas
      and pulling down hard
And I know for sure that I wanted to be watching it with someone else
On the roof of another car
Two years have passed and I don't even know who it was I was
missing

it's not cool to be broody at 22

I'll have a little dainty bump
And look like some Celtic earth-mama
My hair will suddenly be curly and my skin more radiant
What moisturiser do I use?
None: I'm pregnant and glowing, thanks for noticing
Oh everyone will coo and go to touch my belly
With their fingertips to feel his kicks her kicks
I will smile, all proud

Look, look at all the pretty babies that I made
Through my pleasure,
And when they come
They'll sit at my tattooed feet
Looking up
At a grand, red-haired matriarch.

francis bacon's portrait of isabel rawsthorne 1967
or
please get that girl out of my house

A red and ugly face
thick legs
there is no time of day with her only her black frock and the black
car suggests that
she's just come here from a funeral.
She chases hearses.

Blue black cream and messy flesh colours
my eye is held specifically by the flesh colours
they're the shade of what should be inside the skin
making me think of how easy it is for the body look so wretched
someone's rubbed their hands all over her face
and her lipstick is smeared right up to her eyelids.

I can nearly hear the rumble of conversation
she turns a broad back and walks out on thick legs and
there's the purring of motors too. Her feet are so big.
She's left my party in disgrace she is a mess
I think she's broken a wineglass.

Her feet are so big and she's standing in one of the wire garden frames
that roses grow around in summer and spring
but now it cages her, the freak she is.

I don't want to be her friend
she always makes those melted faces at me in the night.

I think she's looking at the lake.
She should go there. Walk right in.

She makes me want to vomit and oh her face and feet and
two
thick
legs.

I don't want her at my party.
I prefer delicate girls with parasols
Neat, clear, and in pastels.

big spoon

teach me how to sleep like you do
with soft lavender snores
as I lie awake beside you wanting to ask you big questions
am I your best friend?
maybe I'll just write it on your body in biro softly so not to wake you
so in the morning you'll see it in the mirror, puzzled
unable to read it backwards
but knowing it's a love-message
from your insomniac girlfriend
best friend

i want to make you jealous of my bed

my bed is gorgeous looking
with ikea sheets
oh the patterns on them look like orange sea anemone on snow
and Christmas lights bought last week in the sales
for three euro
they are the rainbow colours of a box of cadbury's roses
neatly wrapped around the headboard.

i have seven pillows
four blankets in varying degrees of thick
and
two square cushions
one hot water bottle (that burns against my legs so good)
one mute-deaf bear who keeps your secrets
and shit central heating that takes at least two hours to make
lukewarm the room

I have painted toenails on my feet
let's watch a documentary on the small television I got for my
holy confirmation
together lit by the glow of scientific information by the bbc
and cheap rainbow lights
that you shouldn't lean your head against
they could light you on fire and that would ruin the sheets

you wish you were here
you do
you do

untitled poem about how scary growing up is

i lived four doors down from a pre-teen equestrian called lauren,
who had dozens of little prize ribbons stuck
on a corkboard in her pastel and frilly bedroom
i'd envy the ribbons and think to myself
what pretty prizes
how does she get them
i want them
(at this point in my life the only thing i'd ever won
was a selection box at a christmas panto)

she took me to the stables with her one day
i decided i didn't care about dressage ribbons
the stench
the stench and their veiny eyes and white foamy sweat on their
horse thighs
their teeth, somewhere in the small part of myself that was just
discovering vanity
reminded me of my own.
crooked and longer than their faces
tongues the length of a little girl's arm.
the stench, too. the stench.

seeing them and smelling them for the first time
i felt betrayed by all those toy companies
you know the ones
(they were in cahoots with santa claus)
(they showed ma and da how to answer every birthday wish)

they presented me with collectable ponies the size of your hand
in plastics of all the colours that little girls see the world in
minty greens tender lilacs
pink pink pink
with glimmery rainbow manes and a tail that you could brush
and tiny pictures on their round cute pony bums
that when you scratched would smell like bananas or strawberries

or love
they had names like cherries jubilee or lickety split
eyes that glittered with that glorious toy loyalty
i'm your best friend, girl
i'll be there right by your side
they'd sing through their hard smiling lips

no oats or hay or water with dead flies in it for dinner
these ponies ate only clouds and truffles and macaroons
their delicate shoebox houses with crayon wallpaper designed by
my child hands
smelled of potpourri stolen carefully in pockets
from the bowls in nana's good room

for these ponies did not sweat. or piss.
all they left behind was ever glitter, and wishes
and a sudden sense of terrible sadness in your gut
when you realize that was 15 years ago.
and real horses live in stables and are still bigger than you and you
were just too scared of them to learn how to win ribbons like
lauren down the road
now you're 22 and they still look like monsters
and could still kick you to death.

from berceuse

i always knew it would be in an aeroplane that it happened
the rumble and ache of the engine ceasing and before any of us
know it
not me not you not the six year old and his aunt sitting behind us
we're done here and we get to hear that music that we always
wanted to
that loud thumping music we always knew was waiting for us

we won't get coffins we'll be dust from the second we hit the
ground
        we won't even hit the ground
        we are so rock and roll we don't need a funeral
        just one big bang and we're gone out the blue

everything'll go all black and suddenly it's all relaxed like we
always wanted it to be
        and i wish i could weep for the six year old
        you could hear him begin to vomit when the captain said
        OUT OF TIME
        the last thing we all ever heard together,

the noise of our falling out the sky is ripping my brain in two
        so shrill i just know it's the golden fires of hell starting
the rave that welcomes us

c'mon down it's so so hot down here take off your clothes
        dance with us dance with us strip those bandages off one
by one
        unwind them

sparkle sparkle that's when it started, all the parties in hell
waiting for us
       as we disappear from the sky
       in the one tin can in a million that let us down
       and i feel a warming in my soul and a hotness on my skin
       it's so so, mmmm

every heavy lesson ignored burns my body and it feels good, great
       out of time out of time
       their skeleton arms are open wide and we are all invited
to their party
       let's just fuckin go
       it's brighter down there than it was up here anyway

the sound of the bravest thing i have ever done to myself
goes 'clip clip clip'

rusty scissors with a yellow handle
clip clip
against rusty hair
clip clip clip

my eyes wide open as the broken ends drifted
down from my head and into the sink
like furry gold and amber flames
clip

i have been growing my hair long for nearly three years this
november night
when I stand in front of my bathroom mirror
in a green bra and red knickers
vulnerable but the fan-heater is on so i'm at least not cold
clip clip
i coveted every day for long tresses to frame my poor broken nose
and clicky jaw, just like tanya from down the road's
clip clip clip
after baby decades of bowl-cuts like every other nineties kid
making me look like a 5'4 oscar wilde with freckles
in flowery leggings and doc martens
clip

passing into thirteens to eighteens when in a catholic girls' school
i prayed at night to the godesses of teenodm
please britney spears
please christina aguilera
please faye from steps
just make it grow

clip clip

then like some terrifying thunderclap of experience
i was twenty two and had hair that
cascaded
flowed
beautiful woman stereotype word-ed
all the way down past my collarbones and sat happily on my early
twenties breast

clip

only problem was that it carried with it the years of abuse
that boredom and desire for beauty had brought:
peroxide
dye
no don't like that colour bleach it again
grand
dye again
die again
peroxideicide again
so by the time it was long
it was as broken as the silly girl heart beneath the breast it lay
upon
tattered
ragged
tired woman stereotype word-ed

so I take a look at my hair
and a look at my heart
and a look at a yellow, rusty scissors from ikea
and know that I didn't need those broken bits
of what I thought beauty was when I was a child
because in the moment I stand in front of the sink
yellow scissors green bra red knickers
I am happy
Joyous

clip clip clip

murmurings

i want us to go knacker drinking in the dark in the beach by the
suburbs of salthill, lover
and talk about the future that we'll build because we're brave like
that
and I'll mourn that I'll never marry a kennedy because all the
handsome ones are dead
and you're still in love with wednesday addams
which I think is rotten and curl my lip in disgust
and you laugh that mad laugh

you tell me that you'd spend your last tenner in the world on
cherry coke
I hate it so much the smell of it I hate it
you'd pour it all over me and lick it off my sticky body
to spite me
while I scream in protest
(but am thrilled by it for real)

i want us to be teenagers together in baggy clothes to hide our
changing bodies
that we show nobody but eachother
and you touch me first
hell before I even touch me you touch me and I like it
I am not afraid of your young hands

tell you what i'll drink this whole bottle of benylin and we'll see
what happens
it'll be great
if i die bury me in lisa's fur coat and i'll lie still
and never cough with a sore throat from staying out by the beach
with you again

the first time you took me to bed i knew it was the truth
pouring out of your soft disney eyes and into my lust-eyes
as you took me and I let you
even though you weren't a kennedy
and I wasn't christina ricci

punch

I want to punch art right in its face with my bony word knuckles

and kick it right where it keeps all of it's contemporary graphic design
and it's plastic seventies camera from Russia with my language boots
covered in mud, grass and language

bite it hard with my critic-fangs freshly sharpened by cynicism
with eyes cast to heaven

tomorrow I'll quietly apologise and bring it breakfast in bed;
toast with sticky-honeyed high praise and it forgives me as I kiss
it better
with the dry mouth of someone who doesn't know what they want
to be when they grow up

learning is hard
a poem about moving away

The new city is small
Kinda like a sweet baby to Dublin's big daddy
though I know that's wrong these guys have a huge cathedral
daddy city baby city
Galway's a bit like a womb though too maybe it's a mother city
I'll hide up here safe
and grow up up up a little more

Dublin carved me with a blunt knife and
I fought that flat accent but it creeps in with drink and passion
though not many people carry blunt knives

the Corrib's by my door now not the Liffey
sure I live on a street here with a stripclub and a casino winking at
me every time I walk out me gate
Dominick Street's Black Rose across my path inviting me
winking at me to come and have a sly Sailor Jerry
a little dance to the Superfurry Animals

red light lit graveyard of ambition town
but safer in my head here than at home in a suburb on the cusp of
Roddy Doyle country

Parties in this new baby city are in the houses of strangers where
40 people congregate and the door is open and we listen to one
another and join in together

I hope with all my heart you aren't lying to me, Galway. You can
rain on me all you like. I'll let you as long as you keep feeding me
love and rum and safety

Roisin Dubh kissed Eamon Doran one time
It was totally hot, two dirty sweaty pubs in love
but they just... felt... like brother and sister
and couldn't handle it then Eamon died and it was so, so sad

I think he drowned in his own piss
and Roisin stands on the west coast and mourns him
and stays rock and roll in his honour

Had you told me a year ago that I would be a country mouse
instead of a city, city, city mouse I'd have laughed at you hard for
suggesting such a thing
But now back there I am anxiouser than I was before there

Dear Dublin did not hold me tight enough or warm enough or
love me hard enough
it said no to me and sent me far away to educate myself elsewhere
go West girl get the fuck outta here

It was the buildings
the streets themselves
that peered down at me and up at me and told me it was time to
go, get out,
I know you too well and you'll never grow if you stand here forever

And the West opened her arms
and pursed her lips in a welcoming kiss
while I slapped her face for the first four weeks and called Galway,
her pride and joy,
a hick-town
and didn't feel an ounce of peace

because I didn't understand the sighing and stillness
and couldn't hear the rushing of the Corrib lulling me and telling me
the constant rain will wash all the stained anger from the black
city in the east away,
and cleanse me and calm me and fucking chill me to the bone this
wet winter
but still pushing up the edges of my mouth in a smile that warms me
because it is of real, honest happiness.
The kind that Dublin couldn't give me.

we forgot our 9 month anniversary and this never really happened
for ceri

We lay sticky together on a hot morning
I had a soda you had a coffee
My mouth freezing and sweet and fresh
Yours darkened and hot but still delicious
I wondered how it was that you could drink hot drinks even when
it was sweating outside
Does that mean you're an adult
Does that mean we should be adults
Get up you, out of our lovenest and get me another
And another
I am too warm

He rises from the bed and grabs a loose sheet in some useless
attempt at modesty
His voice isn't as Irish as mine
Comes from watching so many movies and Mickey Mouse
cartoons
But his mouth speaks only the truth so I hear no artifice.

He departs and I lie there dreaming of the return he'll make in
five minutes
Six minutes
Five minutes four three two one
He stands at the door
The sheet at his waist like the long white skirt of a wedding dress
A Coke in one hand, the other behind his back

I look over, resisting every urge to stand up naked on the bed
And scream proclamations of my loyalty
Let me give birth to baby boys the shape of you
You are the one one one

But instead I smile at him with half closed eyes and he hands me
the freezing can
And produces a long-stemmed daisy from the folds of his
morningtime haphazard gown

He'd been in the garden
Like a half-naked and hungover man bride
Looking for a present
For his lazy sugartoothed lady groom.

Follies

FLASH PROSE

Follies

ladybird issue

I feel as though my brain is made of ladybirds. Grey matter isn't enough for me - I care not for depictions of brainwaves as blue electricity. I want life there: tiny red insects all a-crawling and making that little noise they make with their wings. I fear of killing them one by one, with too much gin or ammonia or peroxide. They are beautiful and glossed and scarlet and spotted each with dark black and they make my world function inside this skull of mine. A hive of them all murmuring together, seeing what I see and smelling what I smell and creating this place as I perceive it.

Once I was caught. One crawled out of my right green eye and down onto my cheek as I was lying there with him. I did not feel her as she crawled down and sat there upon my cheek amidst freckles on the whiteness. I did not notice her, basking in her newfound freedom for my vision was gauzed over by calm and love. He, however, noticed, stared for a moment and laughed.

"There's a ladybird on your face."

I froze. Not in fear of the insect, no, but more of the consequences of his realization of what goes on behind what he sees of his girl and if he knew the truth and if he knew... he interrupted me tenderly, "...do you want me to get it?"

He positioned his fingers in that shape that precedes a flick. I flinched.

"...do you want me to leave it?"

He hovered there, with that menacing shape threatening the little creature who reclined, unknowing. I shook my head back, ever so slightly. Wires were crossed, he did not understand. With one fell swoop his index finger snapped across the very surface of my skin taking with it, the ladybird, a lone rebel from the contents of my head.

She died on contact. Landed upturned, elsewhere. As life snapped out of her tiny form I suddenly felt an ache behind my right eye. A dark, menacing ache, as though her sisters were mumbling to me through my skull, "You shouldn't have let him do that, sweetheart."

true story

He sat across from me the night I graduated and went, 'fuck them, be a gin supernova,' as I whined to him like a brat five year old in a pink party frock covered in soda bread crumbs that there are people in this city that make me want to punch down buildings with the anger and retreat then and never party again because they make my world so stilted that fireworks are wet and soggy and don't even lift off, not bright alive shooting galaxies in themselves. And I don't have any gin, certainly not enough to be a supernova. I know he meant me to be his explosion in space of joyful and drunk ecstasy but I was so cranky that all I could envision was a dinner-plate with a pile of glitter on it: and a bottle of Gordon's lying on top.

We walked out of that burnt orange and red vegan restaurant after eating our hearty gluten-free dinners (we're not vegan, does that mean we're cheating?) and up Clarendon street in the wet and I pined for a cardigan that I knew I had no time to buy because it was late now and I was leaving for the west again tomorrow.

As we passed St. Stephen's Green a man in a clean suit with a small beard solved a Rubix cube in the doorway of a shop. The sweetest mad scientist, all absorbed in the colourful block of mystery and logarithms in his hands, oh I loved him so much at that moment that I snapped out of my fury tantrum and forgot my cardigan heartbreak, still ginless but stopped my implosion, started my explosion and became a supernova, right there in front of United Colours of Benetton.

the taxidermist's lover

I don't even know who to call. I don't. I mean, I've wanted to
move out. I have. The house is beginning to look like some sort of
natural history museum. All these horrendous stags leering down
at me while I'm trying to read or do a crossword on the couch, or
the revolting jackdaw skull he insists on keeping on a shelf in the
bathroom. He says it's rare. Jackdaws are fucking everywhere and
inside each of their heads is a skull. Rare nothing.

Lately he's started to mix his collection together you
know. I came down one afternoon to find him affixing antlers
from a young stag onto the head of a small rabbit. He just stared at
me and said it was a jackalope and would sell for thousands. I told
then that him he wasn't God but he ignored me. He sold the poor
brown eyed rabbit with antlers for eight and a half thousand
dollars on the internet.

Tonight I was just sitting here on the bed painting my
toenails like any other evening, and I looked at the clock and
noticed he hadn't left his studio. I mean not that he ever leaves
his studio except to get some toast and maybe a Solpadine but it
was getting late and he promised we could...well, you know, it
had been a while. It's been so hard to be with him lately all I can
think of is his hands skinning those poor creatures and plucking
their eyes and... I just can't have those hands on me anymore. I
mean cold hands are cold hands but when his are cold they just...
feel like death is all over them. He'd stopped smelling of Jean
Paul Gaultier and started smelling of formaldehyde a long time
ago. I suppose I don't have to have them on me anymore now.

So I go downstairs to see how he is, try and drag him
away from whatever creature he is moulding or stuffing or
preserving... When I open the door I could hear this noise, this
pouring, hissing noise. It was dark enough, except for his desk,
which always had around three lamps on so he could see exactly
what he was doing. I could see him kneeling on the floor, stock
still. He was vomiting. My own stomach dropped. As I
approached, I could see he wasn't heaving the contents of his gut
but out of his mouth was...pouring, something. It had formed a
pool on the floor. It was sawdust.

He was frozen. He didn't even acknowledge me as I asked him how I could help. I was panicking but not crying, it was frightening to see him this way but as I knelt down in front of him and saw the glass that his eyes had become and the complete stiffness of his face and form I knew that he would not change or get better and this was how it was meant to be. So I got up and left. Just like that and I closed the door behind me and came back up here and I think my toenails are still wet, they've smudged, and some sawdust stuck to them.

I should call somebody. But I don't know who. I've wanted to move out, you see. I don't want to live in a dead zoo. But I don't have to now, do I?

two blindings in two kitchens part 1

Sometimes I'm so fucking freaked at you, mostly you that I feel like taking a cigarette and lighting it in my mouth even though I'm quitting (except at parties) and poking the orange grey flaky ashen burning tip into, then jamming it into my left retina just to hear the hiss of the fire against the slimy green iris that boys always said looked tearful, or prettier by the lights of the chipper. That cigarette would be extinguished, would be smoky but not hot; my wet left eye put it out. Hiss, yeah. Hiss.

So I spark another one between my lips and mmmm I swear I'm quitting then between my fingertips I turn it on myself and in it goes, hiss, into the other eye, the one whose iris is slightly yellower, well, was slightly yellower. Now I am blind sitting in my kitchen on my own. There are biscuits in the press that I can't find now but at least I never have to clap eyes on you again.

two blindings in two kitchens part 2

there is a fat, spherical little bumblebee on the windowsill. as she waits for the kettle to boil, she lowers her head and thinks to herself, oh, what a lovely coat he has, all yellow and black and stripy and furry. and soft, she imagines greedily, envisioning a long coat in those very colours that she would wear, made of the rarest and tiniest creature. a bumblebee fur coat, oh yes, thousands were killed, but this truly is an impeccable piece of clothing. revolutionary? very much so. it's art, you say? I'd have to agree.

he pricks up suddenly his invisible bee ears, feeling a pulse of disrespect from this giantess before him then in a moment faster than she could comprehend he was upon her, digging his acidic sting into the socket of her right eye, just between the eyelids that she'd tried to close. the blink was too slow for him, now piercing the white of her right eye and she screamed as he stole her sight, gleefully.

she tried to get him out, finger and thumb but he eluded her, ready to remove himself and take his chances with her other eye but then it was over, she'd grabbed him with her trembling digits despite her panic and pain. she pushed finger and thumb together with a shriek and then it was over but her eye was stung none the less and she never saw out of it again. the kettle was boiled by the time it was over and she couldn't drink any tea she was sobbing too hard on the floor, the carcass of the wee insect clenched in her fist. she took to wearing a patch over her useless eye in the time that passed and was complimented on it by all the movers and shakers in her scene and there were times she nearly thanked the bee. nature's fist gave me this black blind eye and you know, I must agree, it's rather...stylish.

december

i am lying here because i was not having fun at your party. your friends are dull and all look the same and make me feel like i am the wrong shape and shade and size to be in the kitchen talking about the political weight of contemporary something or other but most of the girls are plain and i think this is funny.

i have drank a bottle of wine and several mixed glasses of other wines. fine wines. fine, fine white label supermarket bob's yer uncle five quid paint stripping vinos. feels like the end of the world in my mouth and the fires of hell in my throat and sweet, sweet stupid and joyful padding the lining of my skull.

i am lying with my hair over the edge of the roof of your building and you don't know i am up here and you would be very angry if you knew i had gone up onto your roof. i don't want to be a supermodel but i want you to look at me the hardest and now i am on your roof and your party is boring.

the feel of icy december on my face is nice up here and maybe makes me soberer and that's fine with me. i decided to lie here because i like the look of our mucky city sky and seeing the stars do their damn best to peep out to see me and say hello, hello you lovely girl, we're interested in talking to you even if nobody in the kitchen is. i wonder what they feel like against fingers and i'd love to reach up and touch them but i know i'd lose my balance and fall off the top of your building and die and nobody would benefit from that. i wouldn't even get to touch them before i fell. it'd be a waste. but this december feeling all over me is good and rich and they are winking through the manky clouds to touch them. i lift my arm.

i lie with half my head over the edge of your roof and my hair billows in the ice-breeze and my right hand will not feel the twinkly teasing lights in the sky and i hear your voice then. shouting. why are you up here why are you up here what are you doing what are you doing.

what am i doing? i am lying on your rooftop. why am i up here? why? i am up here because your party was boring, because there is no wine left, because december's hands through my hair feel better than yours.

fishywish

his chubby infant hands splashed the surface of the tank of water and he was a little unstable on the chair he stood on. his mammy was in the kitchen and this was perfect and he could finally touch them and explore them. his fat stubs of fingers dipped in and slowly followed the mute, silly goldfish. silly fishy. his menacing wee paw followed the unsuspecting creature and grabbed it with an unexpected agility.

he took it from the tank and held it in front of his eyes until it stopped wiggling. he wondered why this was. he just wanted to say hello, silly fishy. silly. the little thing's mouth popped and gaped open mutely. he wondered why it didn't say anything before it stopped moving. it didn't even close it's eyes.

two mornings later his mammy walked into his bedroom to rouse him. she was curious because he would normally wake her by toddling into her room at seven, clambering into her bed and sitting up on her chest and singing to her. he would stop when she got up to make him some cereal. the songs changed every day and were normally to do with the weather, colours, or shapes.

she felt sick to her gut when she saw his bed from the doorframe. it was soaked. she could see his form under the covers, twitching violently. she dashed to her son and pulled the heavy, sopping bed sheet off his tiny form, lying there in the wet.

his eyes were huge and broader apart than they had been. he was lying on his side and she could only see one. they were like huge black marbles in his head. he was alive, certainly. his skin, a strange shimmering orange and flaky. the kind of carotene orange that almost looked like maybe he'd drank too much artificially flavoured juice, except that it kind of shone in the morning light through the curtains. she wanted to touch him but she was afraid pieces of this new skin would come loose in her fingers. his jaw gaped loose, opening and shutting and opening and shutting, silently. he twitched, hands pressed by his side and ankles together. she stared at him in the black abyss of an eye of his that faced her and shook her head. the sickness in her had subsided and she understood, having been the one who flushed his dead pet down the toilet the evening previous. silly, silly boy, she thought. Silly.

unfortunate

It had started as just another series of headaches. Every few days for a week, clustered at either side of her forehead, at the front, just above her temples. She would wake in the morning, crying with the pain and her boyfriend thought that she was suffering from night terrors. She'd just wipe her nose and put on the kettle and tell him she was grand, it was grand, night terrors nothing, they'd be easier than this. She'd pop every pill in the painkilling spectrum and still nothing, nothing could defeat the throbbing, pushing pain from inside her skull. The baby cat looks at her differently, too, since they have started.

This morning she wakes and it is different, the pain is different. Similar maybe to when all the dull annoyance of muted agony that wisdom teeth cause all of us with their forcing their way into our mouths, she feels as though the teeth had broken her gums and were suddenly there in her mouth to be used. Her face is wet. She rubs it and it is red and sticky and it is coming from her temples and there are two, hard, protruding lumps. Like teeth. Head teeth. The cat is on her and licks her damp cheeks and she lets it because it comforts her.

He is gone to work and she leaps from her bed to her dresser in terror at what had been done to her face while she slept and she screams aloud at the white stubs protruding from her skin. It is broken and scabbed and she can feel them pushing even more and she weeps with her hands over her eyes and tears wetting her palms.

The morning passes and by the afternoon she has cleaned herself up and is sitting in her garden and is calm. Cat is on her lap, sleeping. The lumps had grown longer and longer and she had sat in the bottom of the shower until the pain had stopped. Her head felt heavier than usual.

She had dried her hair with a hairdryer and sat naked at her dresser and then went out to the garden. it wasn't too cold that day. Raining softly though. When he gets in, exhausted from work he finds her lying, smiling, hidden in their back garden on the lawn beneath the tiny, lame crab-apple tree with the baby cat. Large skeletal antlers, like a reindeer, protrude from her forehead.

She is no longer bleeding. The headache is gone. Her eyes are wide and brown and her nose is pink at the tip.
She opens her mouth and bleats softly to him that she is happier than she has ever been. She closes her eyes then and the cat opens his.